Copyright © 2015 by Terry L. Morrow. All rights
reserved. ISBN-13: 978-1518725586 ISBN-
10: 1518725589

Walking With The Shepherd

The 23rd Psalm

Rev. Terry L. Morrow, Ph.D.

To the love of my life…Patti

The Lord is my shepherd; I shall not want.

He maketh me to lie down in green pastures:

he leadeth me beside the still waters.

He restoreth my soul: he leadeth me

in the paths of righteousness for his name sake.

Yea, though I walk through the valley of the shadow

of death, I will fear no evil: for thou art with me;

thy rod and thy staff they comfort me.

Thou preparest a table before me in the presence of

mine enemies: thou anointest my head with oil;

my cup runneth over. Surely goodness and mercy

shall follow me all the days of my life: and I will

dwell in the house of the LORD for ever.

Perhaps no greater Psalm has ever been written, sung, read or talked about than the 23rd. Each and every time that I have the privilege to share it at a funeral, in a rest home or to someone who needs the security of God's presence in their life, I am reminded that this is the comforting Psalm that brings so many back to the One that can shepherd them through their hard times.

Psalms 23 still touches our hearts; still calms our emotions; still tells us that our God loves and shepherds us. It has been the one true song that the followers of the God of Israel have turned to through the centuries for hope and compassion. Come with me as I take you on my own personal journey through the splendor and majesty of Psalm 23.

Chapter 1

Throughout time man has asked the question, "Who is the LORD?" Each of us has some form of understanding about who we think he might be. For some, he is so far away from the reality of life that he is not pertinent to who they are or what they do. Others look at him as an over-bearing old man who just sits around and watches us go about our daily lives. He neither cares nor intervenes in any of our affairs. Some simply say that there is no LORD, nor is there a God.

There are many who believe that the whole concept of a higher being is just something that a bunch of weak-minded individuals came up with in order to appease their feelings of helplessness and loneliness. But to the one who has found a personal relationship with the LORD God, they see him as one who loves, cares, provides and guides their everyday lives, and this brings them complete satisfaction.

Picture, if you will, the Shepherd boy, David. He is seated on a hillside overlooking the rolling hills that he calls home. He has placed himself upon a rock and with his instrument in hand, he begins to write perhaps one of the greatest of all songs that has ever been written down throughout the ages. As he puts the words to this new melody, he feels the wonder and excitement of being in a personal relationship with the LORD God, the God of his Fathers, the God of Israel and the God of all creation.

In David's song, he pictures the LORD as a Shepherd. Both David and his Father were shepherds. They understood how the role of shepherding works and they were delighted that the LORD God was leading them in their walk of life.

When we take a look back at Psalm 22, we begin to realize how precious David's relationship with the LORD truly was. Psalm 22 lays out the scene of David, fearful that perhaps God had forsaken him. Though this is a Messianic Psalm,

David is pouring out his heart to the LORD in hopes that he would, "Deliver my soul from the sword; my darling from the power of the dog. Save me from the lion's mouth; for thou hast heard me from the horns of the unicorns." Psalm 22:20-21

There was nothing but pain and death for David. No streams of cool water and no getting through the valley of death. He could only cast himself upon the mercy of the LORD. "Be not far from me; for trouble is near; for there is none to help." (Psa. 22:11)

So, who is the LORD? In the Old Testament, he is known as JHWH-Rohi or Jehovah my Shepherd. This name has been a great comfort to so many who love and follow the Shepherd of David's song. It is perhaps the most comforting name of all his names mentioned in the scriptures.

Psalms 23 is the Psalm that more people turn to during a time of loss, crisis or the death of a loved one. It is the most requested Psalm at funerals and graveside services. It is perhaps the best known Psalm of all that David wrote. This Psalm brings hope and comfort and David, like us, was in need of the LORD's comfort.

David had some hardships in his life by the time he wrote this song. It was the song that declared David's trust and devotion to the LORD like no other he had written.

It is in this Psalm that our hearts are brought close to a loving and caring God. We each seek the love of another. We long to feel the comfort of that love and through this Psalm, we come face to face with a God who loves us and cares enough for us to watch over and protect us from any danger or enemy that might try to destroy us.

The primary meaning of the name, JHWH-Rohi is that of feeding or leading one to a pasture. It can be used to indicate the relationship that a King or Prince may have between his people. Often it is translated to mean a companion or friend. It expresses the idea of intimately sharing your life substance by meeting someone's basic everyday needs.

Exodus 33:11 states *"And the LORD spake unto Moses face to face, as a man speaketh unto his friend..."* JHWH-Rohi spoke with Moses in an intimate way – face to face. This signified a personal relationship between Moses and the LORD. Moses was well-pleasing in JHWH-Rohi's sight. This relationship between them was to be cherished and treasured.

Isaiah 40:10-11 says, *"Behold, the LORD God will come with strong hand, and his arm shall rule for him: behold, his reward is with him, and his work before him. He shall feed his flock like a shepherd: he shall gather the lambs with his arms, and carry them in his bosom, and shall gently lead those that are with young."* This is the relationship that David was writing about in the 23rd Psalm. This was an intimate, fulfilling and complete love relationship between JHWH-Rohi and David.

Not only is he the great Shepherd, but David says he is *my* Shepherd. JHWH-Rohi shepherds each of his sheep. As the God of the individual, he is intensely personal and relational with his sheep. In Psalm 139:1-6, David writes that the LORD, JHWH, the all-knowing God, is personal, relational, intimate and precious.

Once you begin a dialog about the LORD, our Shepherd, you must ultimately ask the next question, *"Who then is Jesus?"*

Jesus the Christ, the Son of the living God, is the Shepherd of the sheep; the JHWH-Rohi of the New Testament. John wrote about him and shared with us the proclamation that Jesus made when he was speaking to the Jews about his power and authority as the good Shepherd. In John 10:11, Jesus proclaims, *"I am the good shepherd; the good shepherd giveth his life for the sheep."* Jesus is all about relationships. He is all about caring. He is all about leading. And he is all about watching over us. Jesus is the good Shepherd.

The Jesus of the New Testament was the 23rd Psalm coming alive. He was the Shepherd of Isaiah 40:11. He was the one who came and took care of his sheep in Ezekiel 34:11-16.

Hebrews 13:20 tells us that Jesus is the *"Great Shepherd of the sheep."* Peter declared in his first letter that Jesus is the *"Shepherd and bishop (overseer) of our souls."* (1 Peter 2:25)

It is good to note that Isaiah 53:6-7 describes the Messiah as the lamb who would be led to the slaughter, and as a sheep that did not cry out during his time of great pain and anguish. As the Lamb of God, Jesus laid down his life for his sheep. We, the sheep, went astray and he followed after us. He took all of our iniquities and the punishment we should have received. He took them upon himself when he died on the cross.

Jesus was a lamb, led by his Father to give his life for us. He truly is the good Shepherd. A good Shepherd lays down his life for his sheep.

This is the great Shepherd that David was writing about. David declared that the LORD was his Shepherd. His role was to protect, guide, correct, love and take care of his sheep. Paul wrote in Philippians 4:19, *"But my God shall supply all your need according to his riches in glory by Christ Jesus."*

Being our LORD means he is willing and able to take care of all our needs. Those needs may include a doctor's bill, financial needs, spiritual needs and everything in between. When life is confusing, he is our LORD. When problems are too great for us, he is our LORD. When we are so worried we cannot sleep or deal with any more stress, he is our LORD.

As followers of the good Shepherd, we have a relationship that should cause us to stop worrying and complaining and start trusting by allowing the LORD, our Shepherd, to have control over our lives.

Chapter 2

The LORD, he will take care of my each and every need because I am one of his sheep; therefore I will never be without anything good.

The Hebrews understood the word "want" to mean that you have a need or you have failed to get your needs met. Why then can we say that we are never in need? The answer is quite simple. It is because the LORD, who is our Shepherd, takes care of us. He is JHWH-Jireh, the LORD who provides.

The word "Jireh" is a form of the verb "to see." Translated into today's language it would be "to provide." Why the difference? With God, to see is also to provide or foresee our needs. The LORD God is an eternal God full of wisdom and knowledge. Thus he knows everything from the beginning to the end. He is the all-knowing, all-wise and all-powerful LORD God. Because he is all of this, he can foresee every need we have and being our Shepherd, he has the means and will to provide for us.

Another word for seeing is "vision." We get the word video from the Latin understanding of this word. God's foreseeing or provision equated to his provision of all our needs.

Because of the fall of mankind in Genesis 3, our holy, righteous and loving Shepherd saw what man would do in the garden and in his ability to see ahead, he provided for our need. That pre-vision led his Son to die on the cross for the sins that we committed in the Garden of Eden.

The word "provision" is a compound of two Latin words meaning "to see beforehand." The Greeks understood then that for God, pre-vision and pro-vision were one in the same. Thus a good translation of JHWH-Jireh in today's understanding could be "the LORD who provides beforehand."

In Genesis 22:8 we read *"And Abraham said, my son, God will provide himself a lamb for a burnt offering: so they went both of them together."* What Abraham was actually saying was, "God will see to it that when we arrive for the burnt offering, there will already be a lamb for us." Abraham believed that his LORD, JHWH-Jireh, would provide the necessary sacrifice to perform the task.

Genesis 22:14, *"...in the mount of the LORD it shall be seen."* God's provision was seen by all. On Mt. Moriah, the LORD God provided for Abraham and Isaac. The word "Moriah" is a kindred word to "Jireh." Though their root words are the same, its ending is an abbreviation form of the name "Jehovah." Jireh then can mean "seen: or "provided by Jehovah." It is interesting to note that Moriah is also the site of Solomon's temple and the same area that Herod built the temple for the Jews during the time of Christ.

In John 8:56, Jesus stated that Abraham saw the provision of the LORD God on Mt. Moriah. Jesus was teaching his listeners that JHWH-Jireh would one day provide the ultimate Lamb of God for

Israel. That lamb was Jesus, the Lamb of God who would take away the sins of all mankind.

The story of Abraham and how the LORD provided a lamb for him was an illustration of how the LORD God would provide for us his One and only Son. John 3:16 states this so beautifully. *"For God so loved the world, that he gave his only begotten Son, that whosoever believeth in him should not perish, but have everlasting life."*

Jehovah-Jireh, the LORD who will see and provide, is the LORD that provided for Abraham. That same LORD on Mt. Zion or Jerusalem, or Mt. Moriah provided the perfect Lamb for the redemption of man's sin. It was the cross that 1 Peter 1:19 said redeemed our souls. It took the "precious blood of Christ, as of a lamb without blemish and without spot" to provide for us our salvation.

Our world is in great need today. You and I are more aware of that than ever before. Where do we turn when we are in need? The Bible tells us that we should not worry about our tomorrows. Jesus taught us that our Heavenly Father is fully aware of all our needs and is more than equipped to take care of them.

Matthew 6:33 tells us, *"But seek ye first the kingdom of God, and his righteousness; and all these things shall be added unto you."* Jesus is telling us to remember that our God, JHWH-Jireh, will provide for our every need; we just need to keep our priorities straight. We need to actively go after God's kingdom. That means that we must first acknowledge that he is our Shepherd. Then we must make seeking his kingdom a priority in our lives.

God's kingdom is the authority and rule for us. We will not be in want as long as we accept the fact that our Shepherd has the controls of our hearts and minds. The reason we will not be in need or want is because we will acknowledge our daily need of his kingdom to rule and reign in us.

Seeking God's kingdom daily is to seek after the character of God that resides in our hearts. When we allow his kingdom to work within us, we are allowing his righteousness to reign over us. The expression of this reign will be seen in how his righteousness controls our lives.

Faith is seen in a person's life by the fruit that they produce. Our character comes out in our conduct. As we allow JHWH-Jireh to take care of our needs, the world will see that we are pursuing the righteousness of God's kingdom. They will see that the LORD is our Shepherd.

⸻

There are things in this life that we simply do not need. Why? Because we trust that the LORD will take care of all our needs. There are things that we do not want. Why? Because we trust that the LORD will take care of all our needs. There are things that the LORD will not give us. Why? Because we trust that he will take care of all our needs. And we believe that the LORD will give us what we need. Why? Because we trust that he will take care of all our needs.

Since the LORD is our Shepherd and we are in need, it is our job to follow him, trust in him and serve him. It is the LORD's job to take care of the rest. It is our job to allow him to be our Shepherd. By doing so, we allow him to take care of us. And that means we will not be in want for anything.

Chapter 3

Have you ever felt a sense or a need for a deeper rest with God? A rest that has many times escaped you? Would you not just love to slow down your pace and enjoy the simple things of life?

In recent history a fascinating phenomenon has happened. Psychologists and sociologists began to proclaim that we would soon have a crisis of too much leisure time. Technology was going to free up our busy schedules and we would find ourselves with not much to do. They were wrong. The simplicity of technology led to more hours of work per week. We now have the ability to bring our work home on our laptops and iPads. These supposedly time-saving technologies did not save us any time. Instead, they drove us to be more driven and more productive. By best accounts, leisure time has escaped most of us, and we are finding that Americans are more tired now than ever before. (Here I am, writing this book, in my off hours, because I have a laptop at my home office which is in my bedroom.)

People are bored more than ever today. They are afraid to spend time alone. They have done all they can to escape from themselves. They thought they had achieved the ultimate emotional fix in technology but soon discovered that it too was just a cold piece of machinery that had no feelings or emotions. What they thought would bring complete stimulation actually brought them complete insomnia. They are restless and nothing is satisfying their souls.

Do you remember what God's original plan was for man? In Genesis 2:2-3 we read *"And on the seventh day God ended his work which he had made; and he rested on the seventh day from all his work which he had made. And God blessed the seventh day, and sanctified it: because that in it he had rested from all his work which God created and made."*

God had laid out a plan for man that was meant to protect him. Rest was given to him so that he would have boundaries or limits to what he should do with his time.

Note that there are two key words used in Genesis 2:2-3. The first is "finished." God had ended his work of creation and accomplished everything that he set out to do. His plan of creation was done and he ceased from his labor having successfully completing his work.

The second key word is "rested." God stopped from his work of creation. He was done. He had come to the end of his work day and it was time to rest. We get the English word "Sabbath" from the Hebrew word "wayishbot." The Sabbath is observed from sunset Friday evening to sundown Saturday evening. It is marked by a time of rest, worship and biblical study. The purpose for this rest was to protect mankind from overworking and getting burned out. And as we know, burn out leads to all kinds of health issues and can ultimately take a person's life.

In Exodus 20:8, Moses wrote down the instructions that God gave him concerning the reason for the Sabbath. *"Remember the Sabbath day, to keep it holy."* It would seem that rest and holiness go hand in hand. In holiness you are to keep things clean, pure and set apart for God's use. The rest that God laid out for us were boundaries that would force us to worship him, honor him, trust him, follow him and rely upon him.

Business can become our god. The Creator knew this and instituted a rest or Sabbath that would make us stop and reevaluate who was really in charge of our well-being. Worship and honor that are given to God always results in a heart filled with peace and rest.

The Psalmist goes on to say in verse two of Psalms 23 *"He makes me lie down..."* How does one find the time to lie down? Again, our lives are so complicated. There is not enough time in a day to take a rest, much less to lie down. So how do we get ourselves to the place where we can lie down? The first thing we must do is to free ourselves of the fears that steal our rest.

Fear can strike us at any moment. Your heart begins to race, your blood pressure spikes, your neck muscles tighten and you break out in a cold sweat. Fear can completely knock you off your feet and shut down your emotions and ability to reason or think clearly. We will typically have the desire to run when this type of fear kicks in.

It is at moments like these that our Shepherd wants us to listen to his instructions to lie down. Running is not the answer. Trusting that God understands our fears and knows what is best for us will help us to lie down and rest.

The second thing that would help us to lie down is being committed to resolving conflict with those whom we have wronged. Conflict is the enemy of rest. Conflict produces restlessness and discord among friends and family. Conflict is only out to cause us pain and hurt. Conflict always sets out to destroy. In order for us to find true rest, we must resolve conflict.

The third thing that can help us to lie down is making sure that there is nothing that might be distracting us from hearing the Shepherd's command to lie down. There are so many distractions today. The news, our own insecurities, no hope, the worries of life, an undisciplined mind, an out-of-control lifestyle, spiritual weaknesses, emotional and physical pain. These can cause us to not lie down and find rest.

The Shepherd of our souls longs to take care of all our needs. In order for us to find the pastures to lie down in, we must allow him to take care of us. 1 Peter 5:7 states *"Casting all your cares upon him; for he careth for you."*

And lastly, you cannot be hungry and find yourself at rest. A good Shepherd will find those green pastures where there is ample water and good feeding ranges. His goal is to have enough for each sheep so that they will be content enough to want to lie down and trust in the provisions of the Shepherd.

The good Shepherd knows what it takes to provide for his sheep. The LORD knows what it takes to provide for us. We all are in need. We hunger for love, acceptance, power, position, relationships and God. It is sad that we have not found the green pastures that the Shepherd has provided for us. It seems that we are always looking for greener pastures on the other side of our life's journey.

I have often called the greener pastures as the "If only's. If only I had a better husband or wife. If only I had better kids or a better job. If only I had gone to college or listened to my parents. If only I had taken that job or married my high school sweetheart. If only I had done what God wanted me to do.

The "If only's" are killers. They cause us to wander away from the Shepherd. We are never content, always searching for something bigger and better and no one thing seems to bring us real satisfaction. But what if we allowed God to lead our life? What if we allowed our hearts to be loved by him? What if we gave all our fears and worries to him? And what if we became content with what he has given us in this life?

David said that the Shepherd *"makes me lie down."* His making us lie down is done by gently leading us. He does this by caring for our needs and guiding us to the green pastures. His making us lie down is motivated by his love for us. He makes us lie down because he knows us and watches over us.

The LORD, our Shepherd, knows that we can easily be spooked or distracted. His desire is that we not worry about the cares of our heart but that we trust him to take care of each one. He wants to take away all the distractions so that we will be able to lie down and relax in his watchful care.

Stop and look around. Realize that your Shepherd has provided everything we need to find rest for our souls.

Chapter 4

In Judges 6:24, we find a young man named Gideon. Israel had been experiencing severe oppression by the Midianites because they had done evil in the sight of the LORD and his hand was against them. The Midianites would often raid Israel's land, steal their crops and destroy their livestock.

One day, Gideon was threshing wheat while hiding from the Midianites. An angel of the LORD appeared to him and said *"The LORD is with thee, thou mighty man of valour."* As the LORD reveals his plan for Gideon, his faith in the LORD grows and his commitment to him becomes strong. By faith, Gideon builds an altar to the LORD and calls it "Jehovah-Shalom." He believed that the LORD would bring victory and peace to Israel.

———————————————————————

Jehovah-Shalom is a wonderful name that has profound effect upon our lives. In Deut. 27:6 we read *"Thou shalt build the altar of the LORD thy God of whole stones: and thou shalt offer burnt offerings thereon unto the LORD thy God."* Whole or unhewn (Shalom) stones were used for the altar.

There are various ways that the "Shalom" is used. In Daniel 5:26 it reads *"This is the interpretation of the thing: ME'NE; God hath numbered thy kingdom, and finished it."* Finished or ended (Shalom) was God's decree to Bel-shaz-zar's kingdom. And 1 Kings 8:61 we see it used as the word "perfect." *Let your heart therefore be perfect with the LORD our God, to walk in his statutes and to keep his commandments, as at this day."* Israel's hearts were to be without sin or perfect (Shalom): to be in wholeness and in harmony with God.

Shalom was also used to depict peace. The basic idea for peace was having a harmony of relationships or reconciliation. It applied to the payment of a debt or even the giving of satisfaction. Often peace (Shalom) reflected an expression of the deepest desire of one's heart.

Perhaps one of the greatest names for the Messiah is found in Isaiah 9:6. *"For unto us a child is born, unto us a son is given; and the government shall be upon his shoulder: and his name shall be called Wonderful, Counsellor, the mighty God, the everlasting Father, the Prince of Peace."*

If you were to visit Israel today and greet someone on the street they will say to you, "Shalom, shalom." Peace is still on the minds and hearts of the Israelites and they are still hoping for their time of peace to come.

We know that when we are left to ourselves, peace will leave us. We become self-centered and destructive. We are quick to become lovers of ourselves and to forget that our love should always be directed to God. This turning to ourselves takes away our peace. We will find that we will be alone and without hope.

The God of peace revealed himself again in the New Testament writings. In Hebrews 13:20-21, the author wrote, *"Now the God of peace, that brought again from the dead our Lord Jesus, that great shepherd of the sheep, through the blood of the everlasting covenant, Make you perfect in every good work to do his will, working in you that which is well-pleasing in his sight, through Jesus Christ; to whom be glory for ever and ever. Amen."*

Matthew 11:28-30 quotes Jesus as saying *"Come unto me, all ye that labour and are heavy laden, and I will give you rest. Take my yoke upon you, and learn of me; for I am meek and lowly in heart: and ye shall find rest unto your souls. For my yoke is easy, and my burden is light."*

Jesus carried within him the very peace of God. That rest or peace we get from him protects us from the enemy of our soul, the Devil himself. This is the peace that can lead us beside the quiet waters.

David is telling us in Psalm 23:2 that God has promised to lead us next to quiet waters. Does not quiet waters make you think of calmness, quiet, peacefulness, rest and relaxation? The problem is, most of the time our lives are troubled, in disarray, turmoil, uncertain and chaotic. The question then is, "How do we have peace in troubled times?" Note the words "leads me" in this verse. We see that the Shepherd's job is to feed, guide and offer rest to his sheep. When God leads us, we can be sure that he will make it possible for us to rest.

Allowing God to lead us is a daily discipline. We know there is trouble all around us. The enemy is looking for ways to destroy us. The truth is, we migrate toward bad things. We are a typical sheep with typical desires and wants. We must allow the Shepherd to lead us to quiet waters. It is his peace that prepares our hearts for our time of rest.

●————————————————————————●

As an average human being who needs lists and charts in order to check off how I am doing with a project, I would like to present to you a "to do" list for how you and I can allow God to lead us to the quiet waters.

First, be honest with yourself and make sure that the LORD is truly your Shepherd.

Second, give him the authority in your life to lead you to the quiet waters. 1 Peter 5:7 tells us *"Casting all your cares upon him, for he careth for you."*

And third, find your real peace through a personal relationship with Jesus Christ. Either allow him into your heart and life today, or give back your cares and worries by allowing the Shepherd to provide you with a place next to the quiet waters.

By following the good Shepherd to the quiet waters, we are allowing his grace to flow through our hearts and minds. Our fears will be taken away and the good Shepherd's presence will reassure our hearts and minds of his peace.

Be sure to find your rest beside the quiet, still waters. There is peace to be found there.

Chapter 5

Exodus 15:2 says *"The LORD is my strength and song, and he is become my salvation; my father's God, and I will exalt him."* Moses is stating that the LORD, JHWH, is the very essence of strength. To Moses, the LORD, who IS, provides for his children their essential needs. He and he alone has the power and ability to meet each and every need.

The LORD God has a way of providing for his children in times when they least expect it. In Exodus 15, we see that the LORD is providing for Israel a second time. The incident arises out of one of their earliest experiences of God's watch care over them. The Israelites had just crossed the Red Sea. They had traveled afterwards for three days not finding any water. It is important to note that on average a person should drink at least eight ounces of water per day. If there were approximately two million people following Moses in the wilderness that would mean that they would need about 16 million ounces of water. That equates to 125,000 gallons per day. We can see why the Israelites began to complain.

Exodus 15:26 tells us that *"The LORD made a statute and an ordinance, and there he proved them."* Their test was, would they listen to God by doing the right thing and keeping his laws and commands? If they did, then none of the things that happened to the Egyptians would be brought upon them. He made this deal because he was JHWH-Rophe, the LORD who heals and restores.

It is here in the story that we see God's provision for his children. At the place where the LORD makes this ordinance there are twelve springs and seventy palm trees. Not only had the LORD made a promise, he fulfilled it. Both their physical and spiritual needs were met at the waters of Marah. What once was a bitter moment for Israel, God turned into a refreshing of their souls.

There are lessons to be learned from Israel's experience in the desert next to Marah. Lessons that directed them back to remembering that the LORD was a God who desired to restore their souls.

The first lesson was their need for healing. Disease was all around them. It is no respecter of persons. It has always been a part of our world since the fall of mankind in Genesis 3. They, like us today, are a needy people and the LORD has been there to meet our needs.

Secondly, they needed a spiritual healing. Sin has done a great deal of damage to the world. Jeremiah 17:9 says *"The heart is deceitful above all things, and desperately wicked: who can know it?"* Man's sin has alienated him from the LORD. We are in need of a spiritual healing. The waters of Marah is a picture of the bitterness that sin can cause in any life. A person's life can become bitter because of the effect of the death of a loved one, or a deep, heart wrenching pain inflicted by a dear friend, or the overwhelming stress and frustration that disease brings to one's body. Each of these is the result of sin.

In Exodus 15:25, God told Moses to throw a tree into the bitter water. That tree brought healing and sweetness to it. The tree was a picture of God's sweet healing that he brought to his children. David pictures God's sweetness for one's soul when he penned Psalm 19:10. *"More to be desired are they (God's judgments) than gold, yea, than much fine gold: sweeter also than honey and the honeycomb."* JHWH-Rohe is the remedy for the bitterness of one's soul.

———————————————————————————

The gospel is the story of salvation that brings us moral and spiritual healing. Jehovah showed his concern for us through his name. His name suggests to us that his attributes are moral and spiritual. And his name tells us of his righteousness, holiness and love.

Jehovah means that he holds you and me responsible for being morally and spiritually minded.

It was through Jehovah's love that our sin problem was taken care of and a healing of our souls took place which took away our debt to sin and healed us of our spiritual death.

What was it that the waters of Marah represented? Marah taught us of disappointment. We were expecting something that would be a quick refreshment, but instead turned out to be quite bitter. We learned that life can be very bitter and that what we believe to be an automatic for us can sometimes turn out to be a bitter pill to swallow.

But we also learned that God can take care of the bitterness of life and sweeten it up with his healing touch. Marah represented our discouragements being turned into hope; unbelief to belief; murmuring to praise; sadness to joy.

Psalm 103:2-5 reminds us to *"Bless the LORD, O my soul, and forget not all his benefits: Who forgiveth all thine iniquities; who healeth all thy diseases; Who redeemeth thy life from destruction; who crowneth thee with lovingkindness and tender mercies; Who satisfieth thy mouth with good things; so that thy youth is renewed like the eagle's."*

David wrote that the LORD, our Shepherd, restores our soul. When the LORD brings restoration to us it is meant to impart new life into our weakened hearts. Restoration brings life back to a slowly dying life. For some, when God restores their souls, he brings them back to the point where they once were close to him. JHWH-Rophe wants us to come back to where we belong. He desires to restore to us a proper relationship with him.

Psalm 42:11 *"Why art thou cast down, O my soul? and why art thou disquieted within me? hope thou in God: for I shall yet praise him, who is the health of my countenance, and my God."* Sheep can so readily be turned over or cast down and not be able to right themselves. This gives a predator an opportunity to attack and kill the sheep. Being cast down is a helpless and dangerous place to be. What can cause a sheep (us) to be downcast?

The first is softness in the ground where they lay. A sheep will become downcast when they rest and roll over on uneven ground. They need solid footing in order to rise up after resting. So, too, a follower of Christ needs to be careful that they do not look for the easy places to rest. Be careful, comfort is not always good for us. Standing upon soft ground can bring hardship and discouragement. We must always be looking to stand upon what is solid and beneficial to our faith.

What we clothe ourselves in can cause us to be downcast. For sheep, too much wool can mean disaster. Rain can mean their wool will become too heavy. Mud and waste can always contribute to the weight, causing them to falter and lose their sure footing. We, as followers of the good Shepherd, must make sure that our outer wool, our old-selfish life, does not cause us to cling to our possessions.

41

Ungodly ideas and the cares of this world may cause us to lose our sure footing.

For a sheep, the best way to fix their problem is to have their wool sheared. It will lighten their load, allow them flexibility and will keep them from many sicknesses and diseases. For us, we need a shearing by God's word. His word causes us to put away all that casts us down. Psalm 119:11 says *"Thy word have I hid in mine heart, that I might not sin against thee."*

Another thing is that sheep must be careful of their weight. Being out of shape can spell death for sheep and a good Shepherd watches to make sure his sheep stay healthy. As a sheep that follows the instruction of the good Shepherd, we must not allow ourselves to become overburdened or even overconfident and have the attitude that we can do this on our own. We need to have a disciplined life.

As the Shepherd makes sure that his sheep do not become downcast, so the LORD watches over us and makes sure we are on good, steady ground where we can be fed and nourished properly.

With such watch care over us, the LORD is enabling us to have our souls restored. In Matthew 11:28-29 Jesus encourages us to *"Come unto me, all ye that labour and are heavy laden, and I will give you rest. Take my yoke upon you, and learn of me; for I am meek and lowly in heart: and ye shall find rest unto your souls."*

In the New Testament, soul or psyche spoke of the thinking, will and feelings of an individual. Our souls are made up of our inner self where we reason and feel. It can be the center of our being where we connect with the heart and mind of God. The question that comes out of this phrase *"He restores my soul"* is, "How? How does God restore our souls?" The answer is found in the good Shepherd. It takes having a relationship with God in order to restore our souls. It takes God reaching out to us. John 10:11 addresses this. *"I am the good Shepherd: the good Shepherd giveth his life for the sheep."* That is it! The only way that JWHW-Rophe truly heals us is by giving us peace. Jesus, the good Shepherd, came to secure our peace. He was the one who died on the cross for our sins. He is the one who takes away the bitterness of life and the sting of death. Restoring of the soul is only possible for those whose soul has been redeemed through faith in the work that Jesus did upon the cross.

Through Matthew 11:29 Jesus told us that, *"...and ye shall find rest unto your souls."* David understood our need for rest. During the darkest times of his life, he found JHWH-Rophe healed his soul. The good Shepherd is still in the soul healing business today. Rest awaits those who follow after the Shepherd.

Chapter 6

Jeremiah 33:16 tells us *"In those days shall Judah be saved, and Jerusalem shall dwell safely: and this is the name wherewith she shall be called, the LORD our righteousness."* (JHWH-Tsidkenu)

Originally "tsidkenu" meant to be very stiff and straight. This gave the concept of how stiff or straight God's righteousness was. This name for the LORD was very significant in the Old Testament.

You cannot adequately translate "tsidkenu" into the English language. The best that can be done is to say that it signified God's dealing with men under the idea of righteousness, justification and acquittal. The Romans represented this concept of justice by portraying it as a woman with a pair of balanced scales in her hand.

The Old Testament depicts God's justice in the same way. Job 31:6 tells us *"Let me be weighed in an even balance, that God may know mine integrity."* Psalm 62:9 states *"Surely men of low degree are vanity, and men of high degree are a lie:*

to be laid in the balance, they are altogether lighter than vanity."

Romans 3:10 tells us that we fall short in our own righteous acts. It took Christ's righteousness to restore our position next to a loving, righteous God. Many of us still try to tip the scale of righteousness our way in hopes that God will show his favor toward us.

Tsidkenu was also used for a full weight or measure toward God in the spiritual sense. Psalm 51:17 illustrates this. *"The sacrifices of God are a broken spirit: a broken and a contrite heart, O God, thou wilt not despise."*

In the 23rd Psalm, David is pointing out how perfect and straight the trail or pathway of God's righteousness is. God is righteous. There is no one who can compare to him. Isaiah mentioned this in his proclamation of how there is *"...no God else beside me; a just God and a Saviour; there is none beside me."* (Isaiah 45:21

The very foundation of God's throne is absolute righteousness and justice. His is an everlasting righteousness that is both teachable and reliable. What we know to be true and merciful, we see in God's righteousness. God deals through his righteousness in everything that we do.

That brings us to an important question. Will we follow his ways, or will we follow our own? The answer to that question has many consequences. If we choose our own way, it could bring us pain, hurt, confusion and eventual destruction. But if we choose God's way, it will bring us healing for our souls, relief from our worries of life, direction for our daily living and restoration to our relationship with God.

———

We all know that there is a cost when we make choices of the soul. Our choices will be directed either by our own concept of truth or we will allow the good Shepherd to guide our paths.

The cost in following God could first mean that we must be willing to love God and others more than we love ourselves. This love will involve our will. 1 John 3:16 declares *"Hereby perceive we the love of God, because he laid down his life for us: and we ought to lay down our lives for the brethren."*

There are actions that love will produce in the life of a follower of God. The actions will manifest themselves in acts of selflessness, self-sacrifice, self-giving and being other-minded. Jesus set for us an example of his love when he gave his all, counting the cost of his life and laying it down at the cross because he truly loved us.

Secondly, it means that we must be willing to get away from the crowds and take a stand for God. Like sheep, people love being together. It does not take much to get a group of people together. One of the reasons for this is that people do not like being alone. They love to belong. But we must be careful whom we hang out with.

Jesus, in Matthew 7:13-14 taught *"Enter ye in at the strait gate: for wide is the gate, and broad is the way, that leadeth to destruction, and many there be which go in thereat: Because strait is the gate, and narrow is the way, which leadeth unto life, and few there be that find it."* Perhaps it is time to get away from the comfort of the crowd and take your stand for Christ by yourself.

Thirdly, our cost could be that we must be willing to give up our rights for the sake of others. This is a hard thing to do. It means laying aside our pride. It means that we will consider the needs of others over our own. This means that there will be a chance that someone will take advantage of us. Are we willing to take that chance?

The key to all of this is found in Romans 12:13-16. There Paul writes *"Distributing to the necessity of saints; given to hospitality. Bless them which persecute you: bless, and curse not. Rejoice with them that do rejoice, and weep with them that weep. Be of the same mind one toward another. Mind not high things, but condescend to men of low estate. Be not wise in your own conceits."* God's righteousness is to be the righteousness of every follower of God.

God's action was that of love. Ours is to be the same. His concern was for others. We are to be about others. His thoughts were directed to us. Our thoughts are to be directed toward others. When we put others first the result will be an honest and complete fellowship with those of like faith. We cannot go wrong when we put others before ourselves. John 15:13 tells us *"Greater love hath no man than this, that a man lay down his life for his friends."*

Our fourth cost is being willing not to always be the one in charge. The Shepherd, our righteous God, wants to be in charge. It is his position to lead. He is the manager of our lives and the director of our souls. Our world is driven to self-determination. We take care of ourselves, try to decide our own fate, plan out our own goals, and do our best to be the master, director and pilot of our decisions. Unfortunately this has not led us to good results.

Perhaps a word of advice from God would help. Notice that David wrote *"he guides me."* It is the Shepherd's responsibility to take us where no man has gone before. We, like sheep, have the tendency to do the same thing over and over again. We take the same path, eat the same food, hang out at the same places and drink the same water. But like sheep, our lifestyle causes us to destroy our environment because we have stayed too long in one place. We are stuck in a rut.

Sheep must be moved to other areas to feed and water or they will ruin the land and cause diseases to come upon themselves. A good Shepherd is looking ahead for the sheep and will guide them to areas that will take care of them. We need to allow ourselves to be led by the good Shepherd so that we will find healthy environments to thrive in.

A problem often arises with us when we get ourselves in this predicament. The problem is trust.

We do not trust the Shepherd nor do we like being told what to do by him. We have the tendency to question him. Why should we follow him? We have become comfortable right where we are. As we look about, it appears that everyone else is doing the same things. Besides, the ground is not that bad, the food is okay and we are just fine, thank you. But there is a problem. We have missed the point of this verse. David wrote, *"He leadeth me…for his name's sake."*

That leads us to our fifth cost. We must be willing to do the will of God and in so doing, we will honor his name.

A good Shepherd is concerned about his reputation. He wants to be known as a good Shepherd; one who loves his sheep; one who risks his life for them and one who will guide them and watch over them. His reputation or name is always on the line.

Our righteous God wants the world to know that he is a very good Shepherd. His glory is part of his nature. And his reputation is shown by what he does for us. This tells us that he will do what he said he would. Titus 1:2 proclaims *"…in hope of eternal life, which God, that cannot lie, promised before the world began."* Our good Shepherd does not lie. If he says we will not be in need, we can trust that he will keep his word. If he says he will provide for us green pastures where we will find peace and contentment in our lives, then we can trust that it is true. If he says that the water is good and we do not need to fear any of our enemies while we drink of the cool waters, then we can trust that what he says is true.

The good Shepherd knows our concerns and worries and is willing to bring restoration back to our confused and misguided souls. This is something that we can trust him for. Why? Because his reputation is on the line. JHWH-Tsidkenu cannot, will not, nor will he ever fail us. He is righteous and holy; true and honest; trustworthy and full of integrity. We can trust him to *"…leadeth me in the paths of righteousness for his name sake."*

Solomon clarified this exact same concept when he wrote in Proverbs 3:5-6 *"Trust in the LORD with all thine heart; and lean not unto thine own understanding. In all thy ways acknowledge him and he shall direct thy paths."*

Chapter 7

Note the change in personal pronouns for the rest of this Psalm. Before it was, "my" now it is, "I."

The sheep are now with the Shepherd. They are away from the herds of the high country. They are feeding at the summer ranges under the watchful care of the good Shepherd.

Have you ever had a mountain top experience? One that made you feel so close to God that you could almost feel his presence? Did his voice speak to your very soul and make you feel at total peace with yourself? Did you wish that the moment would never end? Did you long to stay up on the mountain forever?

Mountaintop experiences are not total reality. There are valleys in each of our lives. For every mountain you climb you must eventually come down. Down to where there are troubles, fears and uncertainties.

I think each of us have felt the mountaintop experiences. We have seen the wonderful moments of God's hand working in lives and even working in ours. And at the top of the mountain, we have felt God's love and compassion. We have also been through the valleys. We cannot always prepare ourselves for them. It is in the valleys that we must trust God and rely upon him to guide us and watch over us.

The valleys can be a life-changing experience. In them we learn to follow God's lead and believe that things will turn around and be better. Some valleys are familiar. We have felt this fear before. We have been here and this time it seems a little harder. The consequences are greater. We question whether we can trust God again. We are not sure that he will come through for us again. And what happens if we do not make it out? Then what?

David said *"yea though."* There was a certainty, a doubtless trust to go through it again. His thought was, "Even when the way goes through the valley, I will trust again." The reality of life is, we will either personally or with someone we love, go through the valleys.

There are many types of valleys that we can go through. There are valleys of uncertainty; valleys of hopelessness; valleys of mental breakdowns; valleys of depression and anxiety and valleys of physical death. For some, their valleys feel like death. They wish for it, hope for it and yes, pray for it. Death can be the release that they are longing for. Death becomes the only way out of their valley.

I appreciate what Jesus taught his disciples as he was leaving this earth to ascend back into heaven. Some of his last words are the greatest of all he ever spoke. Note what Matthew 28:20 records. *"Teaching them to observe all things whatsoever I have commanded you: and, lo, I am with you alway, even unto the end of the world. Amen."* Can you see it? Does it echo through the chambers of your heart? Can your mind comprehend its beauty? Jesus said he would always be by our side. That he would always be walking through the valleys with us; always looking out for our best interests and always there – always, no matter how ugly and death-feeling it got.

In every valley that we go through, God has divine moments for us to experience. Yes, those moments are overwhelming. Yes, we cannot always make sense of them, at least not right away. But it is in the valleys that we learn to trust that our good Shepherd knows what is best for us.

Paul taught this lesson when he wrote to the church at Corinth. His words of comfort to them can be our words of comfort today. *"Blessed be God, even the Father of our Lord Jesus Christ, the Father of mercies, and the God of all comfort; Who comforteth us in all our tribulation, that we may be able to comfort them which are in any trouble, by the comfort wherewith we ourselves are comforted of God."* (2 Cor. 1:3-4)

Our God is a Father who has compassion for his children. This compassion comes from his heart and shows itself by drawing us near to him as he comforts us in the most difficult times of our lives. It does not get any sweeter than that. God cares about us, even when we are in the darkest of valleys.

There can be times when we think that we just cannot go on any longer. The path is too hard and the valley too dark. We long to give up and run for cover. We want to run from every fear and hide from every shadow. Retreat sounds so good to our minds.

It is at these times that we need to be reminded that God's plan is not for us to remain in the valleys. His plan is to get us through them. It may be a hard and long process. We may be asked to learn something while we are there. It may produce the most difficult trial you have ever gone through. But David did write the word "through." That means we start at one end and we come out at the other. Maybe no better for wear, but we do come out.

The fact is God will not leave us at our greatest moment of need. He will see us through to the other side of the valley.

This may have been another valley day for you. It might have been very dark and your fears have gotten the best of you. Often we will feel as if the road ahead is too long and we are not sure that we can go another day.

Be assured that you are not the first to experience this feeling. Many before have found God to be faithful in these dark moments.

David declared God's faithfulness by saying that we would get through the valley. In Psalm 46:1 he wrote, *"God is our refuge and strength, a very present help in trouble."* He could not say that unless he had experienced it. He knew the darkness of the valleys. He came through them and found God's faithfulness at the moments when he needed it.

Valleys can be hard. They can steal our hope and destroy our lives, if we let them. Do not go through your valleys alone. The good Shepherd is there to lead you to the other side.

Chapter 8

Why do we fear evil? David wrote *"I will fear no evil."* As we look at fear we understand it represents being frightened or even terrified at something or someone. The Greeks understood fear as having a phobia or a strong dose of respect for something that is life-threatening.

What is the number one fear that most followers of Christ have? Here are a few thoughts concerning what some of those fears are.

The first reason is the fear of coming across as too spiritual. The backlash to this is that they fear the devil will target them. They will be his pet-project and his goal will be to destroy them. So, if they lay low then perhaps he will not notice them and they will be just fine without being too godly or righteous.

The second is the fear of standing up for their faith. For many, the cost is too great. There is a huge price to pay when they take a stand for their beliefs. The opposition from family members, friends and co-workers can make taking a stand too costly and they fear that if they do, they will fail. No one likes to fail, especially when it comes to their faith.

Thirdly they fear surrendering their personal rights. What was it that Jesus taught in Matthew 10:39? *"he that loseth his life for my sake shall find it."* Surrender of one's personal will and surrender of all control is a fear that will cause them to step away from following Christ. His desire to have complete control is way too invasive for them. They just want some say in what they do; some part in the decision making; some control over what happens. Absolute control is too absolute.

Fourth they fear being punished by God. It is that divine punishment, the "God will get me" fear. This fear can cause them to become legalistic in their approach to service for God. They will become consumed with doing everything right. And if they do not, then they must do it over and over again. For to get it right is to be right with God and anything less is being a loser. And they know that God hates losers. Right? This fear of punishment makes God out to be a tyrant, a merciless ruler who does not care about them personally. He only cares about what they do. Doing becomes being. And being only exists within the realm of doing well all the time.

Such fear locks one into a state of slavery: slavery to their own weaknesses. This fear will drive them away from the loving arms of their Savior. They fear his wrath and lose the ability to feel his compassionate hands lovingly directing their lives.

The fifth reason is they fear that their sins will be found out. They will be found out. They will be exposed for the fake that they are. And that truth is so great in their own minds that they will continue to hide from God, their families, friends and themselves. This fear destroys their confidence in both themselves and the Lord. The punishment that they think they will receive trumps the grace that is already theirs to enjoy.

Fear is an attitude. Our attitude about God, his righteousness, his judgment and even his grace will decide for us just how we allow our fears to rule and reign over our minds. Fear is a sin that is very dangerous. It is alarming how much we allow our fears to control us. They can become life threatening to our spiritual life.

The truth is there is no place for the sin of fear in our lives. The Psalmist said that as he went through the tough parts of the valley of death, he refused to allow himself to be frightened of the evil that was around him.

What evils are we afraid of? Could they be bad relationships? How about bad or evil environments? What about bad or evil thoughts? Some of these have been thrust upon us. Some we invite into our lives. The point is, we need to be careful what we allow into our minds and hearts. These things can either build us up or they can destroy us.

David said *"...thou art with me."* The good Shepherd is always beside his sheep. He constantly is alongside of them, close and walking parallel with their lives. This creates unity in their relationship with him.

Jesus, in John 14:15-16 called the Holy Spirit a Counselor, Advocate or one who comes alongside us to comfort us. The word "Counselor" is made up of two Greek words; para – to come alongside and kletos – comfort or console. As a child of God, the Holy Spirit, parakletos, dwells within us. His role is to guide us, comfort us, help us and be with us each step along our way. As our Counselor or Comforter, he helps us to overcome our fears. His plan is to move us from fear to faith; from turmoil to peace; from defeat to victory.

Philippians 4:6 tells us *"Be careful for nothing; but in every thing by prayer and supplication with thanksgiving let your requests be made known unto God."* There seems to be a five step program here for overcoming fear and anxiety.

Step 1 – Pray. Prayer is turning over to God your fears in exchange for his peace. Remember, there is no fear or problem that God cannot handle.

Step 2 – Supplication (petition). Fear can drive us away from the herd and leave us alone and opened to attacks. Go to the good Shepherd with passionate, earnest, heartfelt prayers. When you have a need, he will help. When you have a fear, he will take care of it. When you have a worry, he will bring you comfort. And if you cannot make heads or tails of this thing called "life," he will help you to understand. And by the way, tell him the truth; he can handle it.

Step 3 – Give thanks. It is so important that we take the time to remember all the good things that God has done for us. Count your blessings often and be sure to recall the times that God was there for you. Stop for a moment and give him thanks. The word "Thanksgiving" comes from two words "eu" which means good and "charis" which means grace. Together we get the good grace of God bestowing it to us his children. David wrote in Psalm 118:29 *"O give thanks unto the LORD; for he is good: for his mercy endureth for ever."*

Step 4 – Get it to the Lord (present). Present it to God in a way that he will be aware that you have come into his presence. Declare it with confidence and make it evident that you trust in his ability to provide the answer that you need. Hebrews 4:16, *"Let us therefore come boldly unto the throne of grace, that we may obtain mercy, and find grace to help in time of need."* Be bold as you broadcast your need so that everyone in God's presence will hear your request.

Step 5 – Go ahead, request (ask). Paul is encouraging each of us to insist or even demand that a specific need be met by God after approaching or speaking to him with respect and honor. In other words, pray with authority; know your needs, but be sure to do it respectfully.

Jesus taught the disciples, *"If ye abide in me, and my words abide in you, ye shall ask what ye will, and it shall be done unto you."* (John 15:7) With a proper perspective comes a proper understanding of God's will for your life. With a proper attitude toward God comes a proper response by him. His response will produce in us a proper prayer life.

Psalm 23:4 says, *"...I will fear no evil: for thou art with me..."* Do not let anything come between you and God. Do not let fear, anxiety or "You" get in the way. Overcome fear by approaching God with confidence and asking him to guide you through your times of doubt and fears. Remember what he has done:

- He is our Shepherd
- We do not need a thing; he takes care of us
- He can be trusted
- He gives life to our souls
- He guides and leads us
- No shadows of death will overtake us
- He is with us all the way through the most difficult times of our life

Therefore, refuse to be afraid.

Lord, lead us.
Watch over us.
We expect that you will.
We promise to follow you
through this whole process.
Help us in our times of fear.
Thank you, Jehovah-Shammah
for being there for us.
Amen

Chapter 9

What brings you comfort? Is it your favorite blanket, your comfortable chair, ESPN sports, that dress that fits perfectly, money in the bank, your family, your spouse or perhaps that vintage car you spent your life's savings on? Comfort comes in many different forms and different packages.

I believe what David is trying to point out here in verse four of his song is that there are two major elements or instruments that the good Shepherd has that truly brings comfort to the sheep.

The first instrument is his rod. Now, I do not know about you, but when I think of a rod, I think of pain. Solomon commented upon the concept of the rod. Proverbs 29:15 says *"The rod and reproof give wisdom: but a child left to himself bringeth his mother to shame."* I always hoped I would be spared the rod but somehow that did not always work out for me.

There are multiple reasons for the rod of the good Shepherd. One is that it will convince us not to go astray from the leading of the Shepherd. Some of us have the tendency to lose our way. It does seem that people are doing what is right in their own eyes. We do not seem to think about God's view of right and wrong. There is little concern for our fellow man. We lack any feelings of remorse. And it is obvious that we do not care about the consequences of our actions.

We need to remind ourselves that what we do, say or even portray will have consequences. We are not an island unto ourselves. What we do affects others and our attitude and actions do matter.

God's rod or word is the extension of his strong arm. It is meant to guide us and teach us what his place in our life is to be. It is to keep us on the path that he has laid out for us. God's word becomes his truth acting out in our lives. We need the action of God's word each and every day in order for it to have its affect upon us.

Secondly, and this is the hard one, the rod of God is meant to be an instrument of correction. The Shepherd's job is to watch over his sheep.

•————————————————————————————————•

There are dangers everywhere. There are people, world events and demonic forces all around us that desire to destroy us and put an end to our relationship with the Shepherd. The truth is, just when we think we are safe and no danger is around, trouble arrives. That trouble manifests itself in hurtful relationships, confusion from undeserving criticism, or a misfortune that you did not count on. All these can steal your feelings of security for the future. When this happens we will need the good Shepherd more than ever to help us and guide us through the storms and difficult times that lay ahead.

Paul reminded us in 2 Timothy 3:16 that God's word serves many functions in our lives. *"All scripture is given by inspiration of God, and is profitable for doctrine, for reproof, for correction, for instruction in righteousness..."*

The word of God teaches us of the truths about his love, compassion, tenderness and grace. It rebukes and brings conviction to us. If it does not, then we did not read it correctly.

Correction becomes the improvement plan of God in our lives. What was crooked becomes straight and what was faulty gets corrected. Have you ever failed? I mean, big time failed? God's word has the ability to bring our failures back in line with him. He will not allow us to stay off course too long. And with correction comes training. Training in righteousness is an act of disciplinary correction by God. His word works to correct our mistakes and curb our passions. Like children, we need direction, teaching, instruction and discipline in our lives. Left to ourselves, we will end up in a dangerous ravine lacking any protection from the Shepherd.

The rod of God's word is meant to change our hearts, attitudes, direction and bad habits. Need help? Turn to the word of God. Need direction?

Turn to the word of God. Need correction? Turn to the word of God.

— • ——————————————————— • —

Thirdly, the Shepherd uses his rod because he actually understands us. With the rod he can bring a swift change of course to our lives. Ezekiel 20:36-37 states, *"Like as I pleaded with your fathers in the wilderness of the land of Egypt, so will I plead with you, saith the LORD God. And I will cause you to pass under the rod, and I will bring you into the bond of the covenant."*

The passing under the rod showed that the LORD had authority and control over Israel. They would be subject to his intimate and firsthand examinations. David asked of the same thing from God when he wrote Psalm 139:23-24. *"Search me, O God, and know my heart: try me, and know my thoughts: and see if there be any wicked way in me, and lead me in the way everlasting."*

We also know that the Shepherd's rod is used to ward off any danger our predators that may wish to attack the flock.

Are not our lives filled with all sorts of attackers? Fear, anxiety, stress, uncertainties about the future and relationships can all be dangerous predators in our lives. Our good Shepherd is more than efficient with the rod to bring us protection. Trust him to take care of the dangers around you. Exchange your stick of pride for his rod of authority. The good Shepherd is much better at fighting our enemies than we are.

The second tool that the Shepherd uses is his staff. It also has many purposes. Each one is meant to provide the necessary protection for the sheep.

Often times the Shepherd will feel the need to bring his sheep together. There is better protection when they are all together in one place. The staff can be used to gently nudge and encourage the sheep to get closer.

With the staff, the Shepherd's reach will be extended and he can get the sheep's attention and direct each one to draw in and find comfort from the others. A couple of knocks on the head, a push or two on the bottom, a firm tap and they will know that the Shepherd has their number and they need to get back in line.

The staff can remind the sheep that the Shepherd is there watching what they are doing and he is inviting them to stay close and not wander off. The staff also becomes a great tool for rescuing a wandering lamb who has found itself in a difficult situation.

Have you ever allowed your stubbornness, selfish will or self-assertiveness to get you into situations that you cannot get out of? Have you ever been so immoral that you could not think of a way out of it? So stuck that nothing was going to free you? So overwhelmed that it seemed there was no hope? That is when the good Shepherd shows up, who, by the way, has been shadowing you all the time, steps in with his well-used staff and picks you up out of your hopeless situation. He takes the time to draw you close, clean you up, reminds you once again that you will be okay, and softly comforts your broken heart.

David wrote *"...thy rod and thy staff they comfort me...."* The Shepherd may need to tap you every once in a while. He may even need to tap you on the shoulder or thump you on the head. But he does all this because he loves you. It is reassuring to know that the good Shepherd stands with his rod and staff in his hand ready at any moment to take care of any and all needs we might have.

Chapter 10

During the summer months, the Shepherd takes his sheep to a plateau where the weather is much cooler. The grass will be lush and green and the mountain waters will be cool and refreshing.

It is the responsibility of the Shepherd to go before his sheep and survey the land of the plateau. He may have done so when there was bad weather but his goal was to find the best location when spring time came around. Camp would be set up and the area would be cleared of any plants or weeds that could bring potential harm to his sheep. It is his priority to provide a safe and peaceful environment for the sheep so that their health and security during the spring and summer months will go well for both them and himself.

The picture here is that of God our Shepherd. His goal is to provide a safe and peaceful life for us so that we will grow stronger in our relationship with him.

Let us take another look at the different names of God that David has shown us through the role of the LORD God being our good Shepherd.

- ❖ Jehovah – Rapha: "The LORD who heals"
    - – When we are sick the good Shepherd brings healing to us
- ❖ Jehovah – Shammah: "The LORD who is there"
    - – We are never alone
    - – The LORD is always by our side
- ❖ Jehovah – Tsidkenu: "The LORD our righteousness"
    - – When we do not feel like we measure up to God's standards, he declares us righteous
- ❖ Jehovah – Jireh: "The LORD will provide"
    - – We have no needs because the LORD provides for us
- ❖ Jehovah – Shalom: "The LORD our peace"

- Do not let anything rob you of God's peace
- ❖ Jehovah – Raah: "The LORD is my Shepherd"
  - The LORD guides us and watches over us

Each of these names for God shows his continual watch care over his sheep. As the good Shepherd, David says that the LORD provides or prepares a table for us his sheep. This means that first he has taken the necessary time to get the table ready. It is not thrown together at the last minute. His work is top notch and geared specifically to our needs. He has done everything necessary so that we will be cared for. There is nothing to be feared because this place of rest and peace has been created just for us.

Jesus spoke of heaven in the same way when he taught his disciples of his plans for them in the future. John 14:2, *"In my Father's house are many mansions: if it were not so, I would have told you. I go to prepare a place for you."*

Secondly it means that the LORD has put a lot of his love and compassion behind his preparations. Each year America celebrates Thanksgiving. It is a time when families and friends gather to celebrate all the good things that have taken place in their lives.

For many, it is a time of giving thanks to the LORD for all of his blessings. But before that day takes place there is a lot of preparation for the turkey dinner. Time needed for cleaning and cooking are underway days before the family arrives. There are tables to set, bathrooms to clean, floors to mop, yards to manicure and laundry to do. All of this preparation is so that when our families arrive they will feel comfortable and at home.

That is a wonderful picture of what the LORD said he was doing in John 14. Soon all will be ready and we will arrive at the feast, greeted by our Savior who will welcome us into his home.

Thirdly it means that the LORD has put the right things there for us. They may not be what we want, nor will it always be our favorite dish. But what is there is just for us. It may not make any sense and it may not seem right, but we will have to trust that God knows what he is doing. All that is happening is for our good and what is on the table is exactly what we need.

Fourth it means that the LORD has put on the table all the nourishment that we will ever need. God's word will bring to us all that we need for our soul food. 1 Peter 2:2 reads, *"As newborn babes, desire the sincere milk of the word, that ye may grow thereby."* The LORD wants us to feast upon his word. It is what brings true satisfaction to our souls.

Fifth it means that the LORD will bring about growth in our lives. When we eat right, we grow right. When we partake of the goodness of the LORD, our lives are blessed and we are nourished properly. This is the dinner table, not the snack bar. It is at the dinner table that our appetites are satisfied, growth takes place and spiritual nutrition happens.

Sixth it means that the LORD's table is where our family gathers. Here we spend time fellowshipping and enjoying each other's company. Here we learn the heart of our Shepherd and we allow him to bring calm to the table.

We share our lives, our hopes and our dreams at the table of the LORD. We sense the love of our Shepherd here and we understand what it means to belong to the family of God. Here, at the LORD's table, we find our security.

What is so unique about this whole scene is that it takes place in the presence of our enemies. It is a realization that all around us our enemy is out to destroy this wonderful setting. Psalm 91:2-3, *"I will say of the LORD, He is my refuge and my fortress: my God; in him will I trust. Surely he shall deliver thee from the snare of the fowler, and from the noisome pestilence."*

Finally as we think about this table that the LORD has prepared the question of who is invited comes up. David made it clear that he was invited, *"...thou preparest a table for me..."* This wonderful place of fellowship, peace, comfort and nutrition was put together for David, one of the LORD's sheep. Like David, those who are the LORD's sheep will enjoy this wonderful table.

The LORD told the disciples that he was going to prepare a place for them. John 1:12 teaches us of the relationship that is built with the Shepherd when we receive Christ into our lives. *"But as many as received him, to them gave he power to become the sons of God, even to them that believe on his name."*

As with David, the table is offered to us and we are granted the privilege of dining with the good Shepherd. The LORD has prepared a wonderful table for his sheep. There they find safety, fellowship and there their needs are met.

Chapter 11

The word "sanctify" in the Old Testament means to dedicate a specific article for service to a god or the God. Once it is "sanctified" that object becomes holy. In Leviticus 20:7-8, the LORD spoke to Moses and told him to sanctify himself and be holy because, *"I am the LORD your God* (JHWH-M'Kaddesh)*, the LORD who sanctifies you."* This name is one of the most important names of God. It truly expresses the character of God and his requirements of his people.

Being holy unto the LORD meant that one set themselves apart or separated themselves totally unto the LORD. Here are a few examples of how this word was used:

- Genesis 2:3 the LORD sanctified the Sabbath
- God sanctified the camp of Israel
- Mt. Zion was sanctified
- The city of Jerusalem was set apart unto the LORD

–   The altar, the Tabernacle and the
    Temple with all of its articles were
    sanctified unto the LORD

The word that was frequently used for both the Tabernacle and the Temple was "mikdash." It meant a sacred place such as the Temple or a sanctuary. It is very similar to the name JHWH-M'Kaddesh. The Temple was set apart for the specific purpose of worshipping the LORD and for housing his presence.

Perhaps the most important thing about sanctification is that in practicing it we learn to understand God more. 1 Samuel 2:2 states, *"There is none holy as the LORD: for there is none beside thee: neither is there any rock like our God."* The most fundamental, most solemn and most impressive of all the attributes of God is his holiness.

God is holy and separated from all moral defilement. God hates sin because it angers him.

Hebrews 12:29 says, *"For our God is a consuming fire."* He will burn away all sin and correct each of us so that we will live sanctified lives. If it were not for God's grace, his righteous holiness would eliminate us from his very presence.

God is holy and gracious at the same time. His grace includes his goodness, kindness, mercy and love without which we would be suffering his full wrath.

David wrote that the LORD anoints our head with oil. There are two effects of God's anointing of oil upon our head. First, the anointing sets us apart (sanctifies us). 1 Peter 1:15 tells us *"But as he which hath called you is holy, so be ye holy in all manner of conversation."* Ephesians 1:4 says, *"According as he hath chosen us in him before the foundation of the world, that we should be holy and without blame before him in love."* On the basis of our salvation in Jesus Christ, we are now set apart or sanctified and made holy in Jesus.

The second effect of God's anointing results in us having the Holy Spirit's power come upon us. Paul taught us in Ephesians that when Christ comes into our hearts to dwell (tabernacle), we would be able to understand and know the love of Christ. This knowledge would bring fullness to our hearts and minds. That filling would enable us to do, *"...exceeding, abundantly above all that we ask or think, according to the power that worketh in us..."* Ephesians 3:20. A follower of the good Shepherd is now to live by the Holy Spirit's power. That is to be a life of sanctification – a setting apart of ourselves for worship of our God.

Our bodies are to be sanctified unto the LORD. Paul wrote to the believers in Rome and challenged them to live a life that is wholly committed to sanctification. Romans 12:1 says *"I beseech you therefore, brethren, by the mercies of God, that ye present your bodies a living sacrifice, holy, acceptable unto God, which is your reasonable service."*

This walk of life or the setting apart of ourselves unto the LORD is done through the Holy Spirit as he anoints our head with oil.

Chapter 12

What makes us afraid of tomorrow? It seems we spend a lot of time worrying about the future. Matthew 6:34 states, *"Take therefore no thought for the morrow: for the morrow shall take thought for the things of itself. Sufficient unto the day is the evil thereof."*

Worrying about tomorrow takes away the joys of today. Today was given to us as a gift from God. Do not miss the wonder and awe of that gift. And do all you can not to borrow from tomorrow. You will end up not having much to enjoy down the line.

⎯⎯⎯⎯⎯⎯⎯⎯⎯⎯⎯⎯⎯⎯⎯⎯⎯⎯⎯⎯

We worry because we cannot see what is ahead. What if it hurts us? What if it costs too much? What if I lose? What if they leave me? What if I do not make it? What if...

Do not allow the "What ifs" to steal your time, joy, love and peace. David wrote, *"Surely goodness and mercy shall follow me all the days of my life."* Knowing that God's goodness and mercy are with us each step of our life's journey makes our hearts feel at ease. It takes away our fears of tomorrow. It slows our mind down and eases our anxious heart. It helps us to make sense of whatever this day or tomorrow holds. We will then be able to say that we feel restful and content inside.

There are multiple reasons for not being afraid of our tomorrows. Here are two simple ones that might encourage you to trust in the good Shepherd for your tomorrows.

1. The Shepherd is watching over you.

Since God is good, he will watch over you. Psalm 145:9, *"The LORD is good to all: and his tender mercies are over all his works."*

The LORD has promised his protection. What does it mean that his goodness will follow us? It means he will run after you and chase you down. Nothing will stand in the way of God touching you with his goodness.

Have you ever had disappointments in your life? God was there. He cared about you in your darkest hour. His goodness was revealing itself to you.

At times it can be difficult to see God's goodness. It can feel like it is hidden from us. It can feel as though we are on our own. It can often appear that bad things happen even when we are doing well. It may not be until much later in our lives that we can look back and see how God worked and provided his goodness to us.

You and I may not feel as though anything good is happening. We might not even think that any good will come of the situation that we find ourselves in. But know that God's goodness is there. Psalm 91:14-16, *"Because he hath set his love upon me, therefore will I deliver him: I will set him on high, because he hath known my name. He shall call upon me, and I will answer him: I will be with him in trouble; I will deliver him, and honour him. With long life will I satisfy him, and shew him my salvation."*

2. Not only has God promised his goodness, but he always promises his mercies will follow us as well.

What is mercy? Mercy is God's grace in action. It is his kindness and favor being expressed to his objects of love. Mercy covers the imperfections of imperfect beings. It lifts them up when they fall before a holy God. It covers their sins. It knows when they fail and yet it never calls them a failure. Mercy is not giving them what they know they deserve. Mercy is giving them what they know in their hearts they do not deserve.

Sometimes we think that God is out to get us. No matter what we do, we feel as though he only sees the worst in us. Psalm 103:10-11 reminds us, *"He hath not dealt with us after our sins; nor rewarded us according to our iniquities. For as the heaven is high above the earth, so great is his mercy toward them that fear him."*

How then should this affect our feelings about the future? One thing we can do is stop and remember God's mercy and grace. Remember that your sins are taken away, your doubts are removed and your relationship with God is restored.

When we go through the rough times of life, David said that the good Shepherd would be with us. He wrote, *"...goodness and mercy shall follow me all the days of my life."* That means to the very last breath that we take. God will be with us to the very last moment of our lives. He will not, cannot, no, not ever stop following after us.

The LORD's mercy and goodness is on us each and every day of our lives. That tells us that even when we are sick, he is there. Through our depression and anxiety, he is there. When we are lonely and afraid, he is there. When life is hard and overwhelming, HE IS THERE!

We will never face this life alone. You may not feel him, you may not know it in your mind and you may not even understand it. But one thing is for sure, God is there.

Note the word "Surely" in this verse. The Hebrew people used it to mean that something was for certain. You indeed knew it would happen. In English it means to be relaxed or to trust. You would know that you could trust in what you just learned and that knowledge took away your fears or panic.

We may doubt, but God says, "Surely." We may have fears, but God says, "Surely." We may run and hide, but God says, "Surely." We may say that we cannot trust him, but God firmly says, "Surely." Our world may fall apart all around us and it may seem there is no end to this mess we call our life, but God says, "Surely."

Looking back upon this Psalm helps us to see God's love and mercy. It helps us to understand his goodness. What we can hear in this song of David is his contentment and satisfaction with the good

Shepherd. Comfort and assurance jumps off the pages at us and we run for protection and daily strength to the One who is constantly by our side.

Psalm 23 is telling us to take our concerns and give them to the good Shepherd. We are to take our fears and deposit them into his strong, firm hands. This song tells us to take our unknowns and replace them with his plans and thoughts for us. The "I" is replaced with "Him." In "Him", "I" becomes surrounded by "Him." As his sheep, you and I are covered with his goodness and mercy. That coverage protects us from our enemies.

Chapter 13

What brings your yesterdays and todays together? It is your tomorrows. David ends one of the greatest songs ever written by saying *"...and I will dwell in the house of the LORD for ever."* The Apostle Paul said it this way in 2 Corinthians 5:1, *"For we know that if our earthly house of this tabernacle were dissolved, we have a building of God, an house not made with hands, eternal in the heavens."*

Forever can be defined as the past and future coming together. It is time without end. 2 Corinthians 4:18 says *"While we look not at the things which are seen, but at the things which are not seen: for the things which are seen are temporal; but the things which are not seen are eternal."* Forever transcends time and space. Forever is forever.

One of the greatest passages of the Bible that helps us to understand the wonder of forever is found in 2 Corinthians 5:6-8. Some key words in this passage are:

- "Always confident" (courage)
- "Know" (able to comprehend)
- "Live by faith" (trust)

In verse 6 of Psalms 23, David uses the word "dwell." It meant that one was going to settle down and remain in a place for a considerable amount of time. The Apostle Paul had the same idea when he wrote to the church at Ephesus. *"That Christ may dwell in your hearts by faith; that ye, being rooted and grounded in love..."* Ephesians 3:17

David used the word dwell to mean that heaven, where the house of the LORD is, would be where he would one day dwell forever.

Death is not the end but the beginning of forever. We will find ourselves at home there. No more wandering through this life. Whatever we may think heaven is, one thing is sure, we stop there forever.

Notice that David says, *"I will."* This means there is no doubt in his mind of heaven. There is no wishing of it and no maybes it will occur. David knew in his heart that heaven was the final destination for him. He had this hope during the greatest crisis of his life.

After the death of his son, who was the first born child of his immoral relationship with Bathsheba, David spoke of his trust and belief in heaven. 2 Samuel 12:23 reads, *"But now he is dead, wherefore should I fast? Can I bring him back again? I shall go to him, but he shall not return to me."*

David was not just willing heaven to happen, he knew it would. It was certain and the ability to do it was there. David knew, after all God had done for him, that heaven was his and his son's final destination. Heaven is God's way of showing us his love and plan for our eternity.

Life will bring many disappointments. Our journey may make some tough turns. The shadows may cover our walk through the valleys. And it may appear that we are being led nowhere. David wanted to remind us that God has prepared a table for us. He will lead us through the deepest of valleys. He is ever watching over us, protecting us from the enemies around us.

David's final dwelling place was in the house of the LORD. What is it about God's house that brings us comfort? Could it be that we just feel a sense of belonging there? Perhaps it is our feeling of worthiness.

We are somebody to God. Peter wrote that we are a special people to the LORD. *"But ye are a chosen generation, a royal priesthood, an holy nation, a peculiar people; that ye should shew forth the praises of him who hath called you out of darkness into his marvellous light."* 1 Peter 2:9

God's house in heaven will be a wonderful place of restoration to our souls. Relationships will be restored. Devastated lives will be reclaimed.

Confusion will be replaced with clarity. God's love will be revealed to us in a more personal way and the tears and sorrows of this life will be wiped away.

The place we call heaven, David understood as the house of the LORD. It is the home of the good Shepherd. Our Shepherd is our companion and friend. He is personally a part of our lives. As his sheep, he watches over us and cares for us.

The Shepherd has not only promised to take care of us, but to also provide a dwelling place for us. No more going back and forth to different pastures. No more lousy winter days. No more scorching heat. No more bugs and flies. And no more enemies chasing us around trying to take our lives. Heaven is home sweet home. It is forever and we will never have to leave.

As you think about your future and contemplate your tomorrows, do not let fears arise in your heart. Do not allow worry to lead you away from the good Shepherd. Replace doubt with an understanding of the Shepherd's commitment to taking care of you. You can either face your tomorrows with the help of the LORD, your Shepherd, or you can face them alone.

———————————————————————————

As the good Shepherd, he meets our needs, takes care of our loneliness, restores to us hope, and provides a clear understanding of our future.

As the good Shepherd, he guides us. After the valleys we find green pastures. When we are hurt, he applies the oil of the Spirit and takes away our pains. What else would a sheep need?

Perhaps the best way to sum up this wonderful Psalm of David is to say, "LORD, guide us, provide for us and care for us. You are everything that we need."

The LORD is my Shepherd.

Made in the USA
Charleston, SC
13 May 2016